The First Time I Laid Eyes On You

by Elder Mary Quick

Illustrations by Torrance Bass

AuthorHouse™
1663 Liberty Drive
Bloomington, IN 47403
www.authorhouse.com
Phone: 1-800-839-8640

Published by AuthorHouse 11/11/2014

ISBN: 978-1-4969-5131-1 (sc)
ISBN: 978-1-4969-5130-4 (e)

Library of Congress Control Number: 2014919890

This book is printed on acid-free paper.

authorHOUSE®

ACKNOWLEDGEMENT PAGE

KJV

Scripture quotations marked KJV are from the Holy Bible, King James Version (Authorized Version). First published in 1611. Quoted from the KJV Classic Reference Bible, Copyright © 1983 by The <u>Zondervan</u> Corporation.

Dedicated to all the Parent as a reminder of the first time you laid eyes on each of your children and how they grew from infant to adult.

Remember the joy they brought you.

And to my children Aja Grice, Shatrece Whitfield, David Grice and to my grandchildren, Nana also remembers the first time she laid eyes on you and held you in her arms and looked into your eyes Jakai, Jasmine, Azaryia, Ivan and Londyn too.

I remember the first time I laid eyed on you. It was in the doctor's office, on this little machine that took pictures of you.

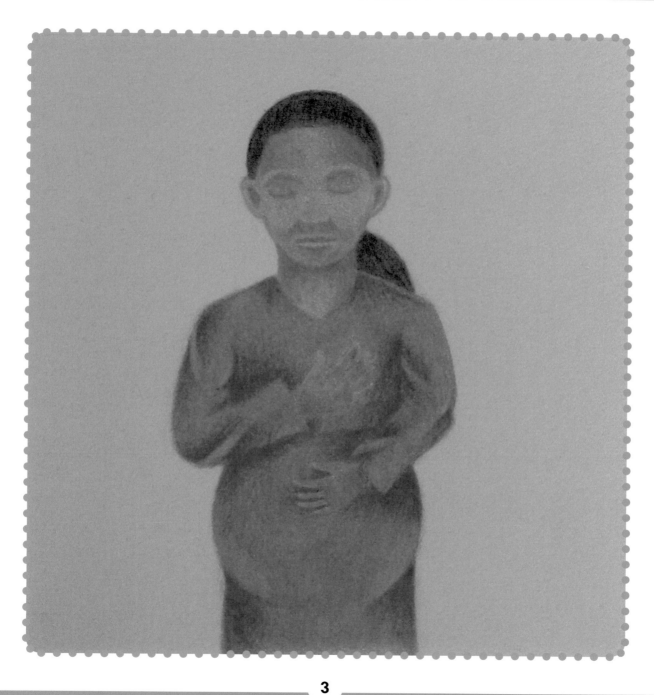

3

Oh, how my soul leaped for joy. Just to know that God took time to make someone as special as you.

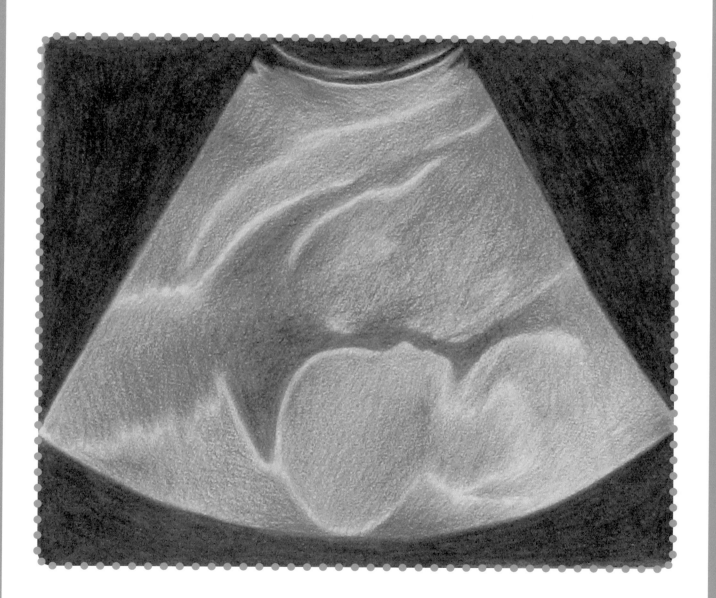

Your picture showed tiny forms of your hands, legs, arms, oh yes and your head too. That was the first time I laid my eyes on you.

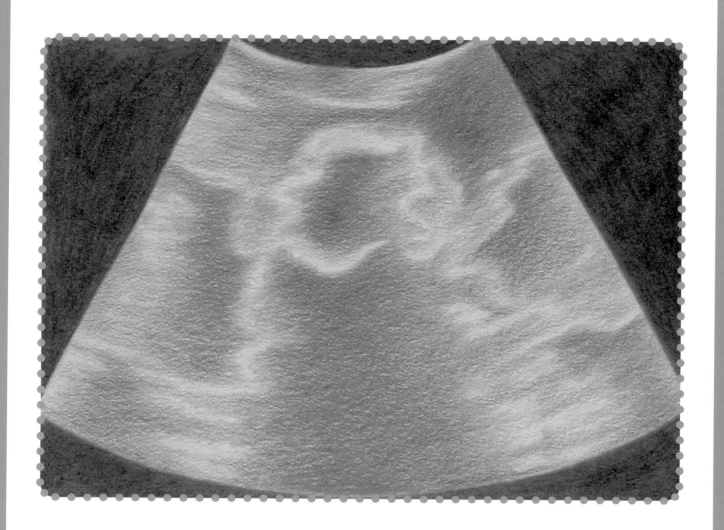

But the greatest thing for me, was to hear your little heart beat as it went thump, thump, thump…

The first time I laid my eyes on you.

When it was time for your delivery, Daddy drove the car to the hospital. They put me in a delivery room.

As I lay still with urgency for your arrival, my mind wondered what you look like and the color of your hair and eyes.

Then the doctor would come in from time to time to check and see if I was ready.

When the time came, they rolled in their machine.

One, two, three… Here comes the baby. Daddy cried as he held my hand. The doctor had to tap you a few times so that you would cry. He had to make sure everything was alright.

Did you know in the Bible it talks about a baby names Jesus and how His birth excited the world and how he grew up doing the will of his father, which in Heaven above. It also talks how miracles were formed and how He died for the sins of this world because He loved us so much.

His mother was a very blessed women (mother) to have been chosen to carry our Lord and Savior Jesus Christ.

"Let the little children come to Me, And do not forbid them, for such is the kingdom of Heaven and he laid His hand on them and departed from there."

Matthew 19:14-15

Meaning that even a child can follow Christ by contrast to their simple obedience.

After the nurse dressed the baby in the blanket, she laid the baby beside me. I counted your fingers and toes making sure that were all there. This was something my mother said I should do. She remembered the first time she laid her eyes on me.

I cried and thanked God for taking time to make someone as special as you.

What joy was in our eyes as we held you in our arms and talked to you.

The next morning, the nurse came in to show me how to care for you once we went home.

It was going to be a lot of activity there. From bathing, feeding, changing and most of all just loving you.

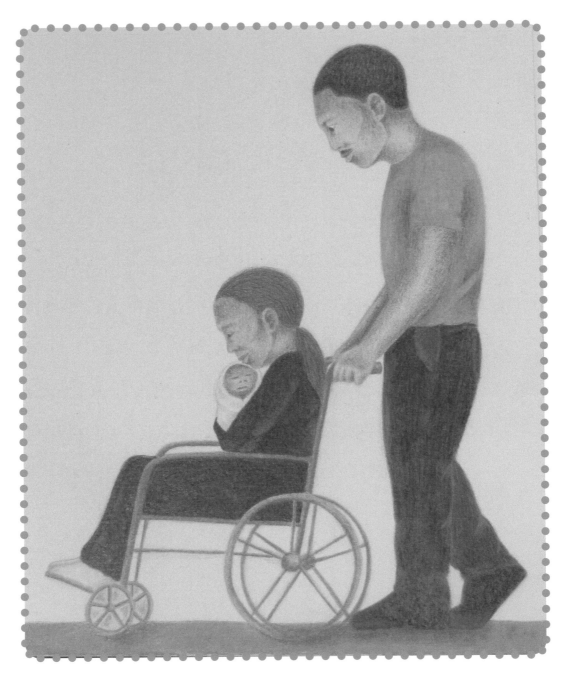

After the 3rd day at the hospital, it was time for baby and mommy to go home. Daddy came to pick us up and off we went. The 1st night you slept really well, just knowing the love and warmth we had right in our home.

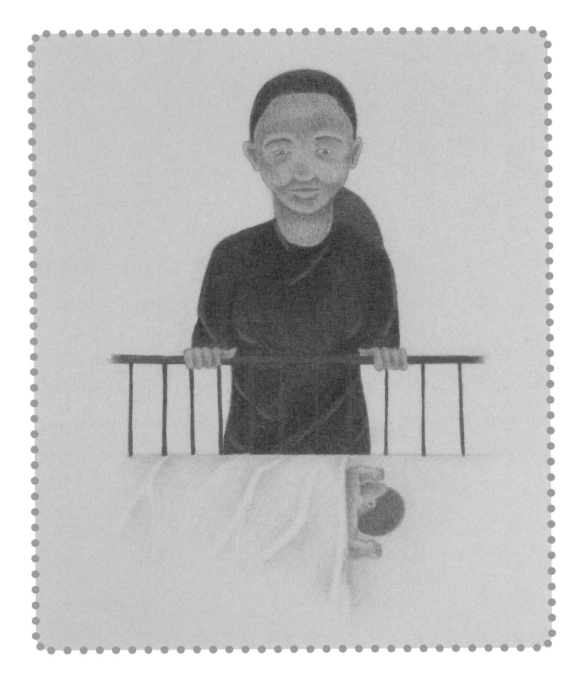

I came in your room throughout the night to check in on you.

Remembering the first time I laid on you.

You learned to crawl from one end of the home to the other end. How excited were you. As for me, I was still remembering the first time I laid eyes on you.

You grew up so fast, learning to walk. Talking step after step, falling then crawling and getting back up to try it again.

On your first birthday, we got you a cake. It was so much fun watching the mess you would make.

Time passed quickly. Now you are two and off to daycare.

Everyday you cried about a week, thinking I wasn't coming back for you. It hurt me so to have to leave. Soon all your crying and all your fear turned into nothing but cheers... but still I remember the first time I laid eyes on you.

You turned three, then four, now five you are. This is kindergarten time, here you learn even more reading and writing your name. Daddy was so proud to see his little baby developed into their own way.

We still remember the first time we laid eyes on you.

Six, seven, eight and nine. Now you are ten, I would do it all over again. Remembering the first time I laid eyes on you.

Now you are in high school and it came with the many pressures within.

But God said you would win each and every time you called on him.

College time is here and off you must go. Daddy and I are so proud of you because you made it through. Sometimes it was rough and many times we didn't agree, but it all paid off.

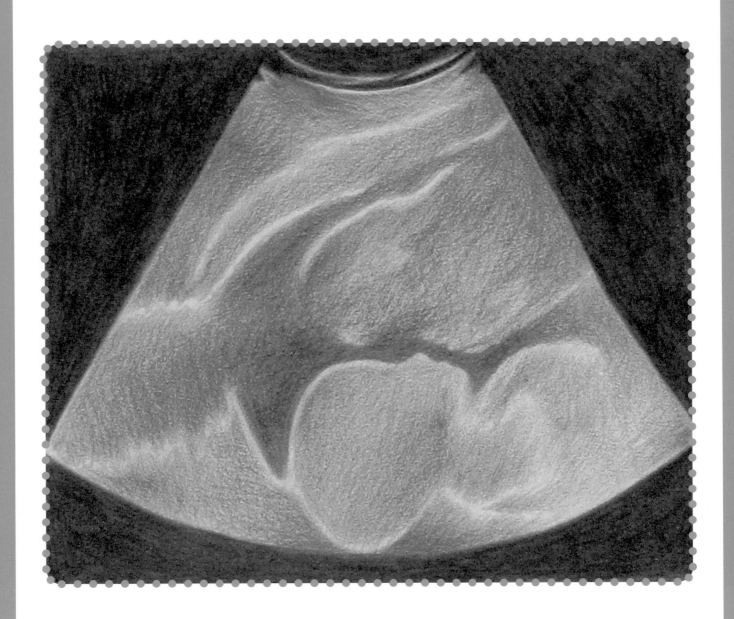

Looking back now and I still remember the first time I laid eyes on you, I thanked God. For it was He who took the time to make someone as special as you.

Thank you my Lord and Savior for all the blessings you have instilled in me as a mother. There were so many times when I didn't think I could do this job, but I remember the scripture you gave me.

Train up a child in the way he should go: and when he is old, he will not depart from it."

Proverbs 22:6

Meaning: When a child has grown up as a mature adult, they will not forget the training that was instilled in them. If they stray away, the child will return home some day.

Elder Mary Quick is a passionate woman who loves the Lord. She is the President of Healing & Restoration, a non-profit organization for women. She is also the owner of Faith's Maid Service of Thomasville, NC. Called by God to spread the gospel, Elder Quick is an ordained minister with the Ministry of Fullness Word of Faith, Inc. under the leadership of Pastor Olivia Allen. She has already written and published her autobiography, The Overcomer From Past to Present. Elder Quick resides in North Carolina with her husband and family.

Printed in the United States
By Bookmasters